A2 Economics
UNIT 4

Edexcel

Unit 4: Industrial Economics

Russell Dudley-Smith

Philip Allan Updates
Market Place
Deddington
Oxfordshire
OX15 0SE

Orders

Bookpoint Ltd, 130 Milton Park, Abingdon, Oxfordshire, OX14 4SB
tel: 01235 827720
fax: 01235 400454
e-mail: uk.orders@bookpoint.co.uk
Lines are open 9.00 a.m.–5.00 p.m., Monday to Saturday, with a 24-hour
message answering service. You can also order through the Philip Allan
Updates website: www.philipallan.co.uk

© Philip Allan Updates 2002

ISBN-13: 978-0-86003-881-8
ISBN-10: 0-86003-881-5

This Guide has been written specifically to support students preparing for the
Edexcel A2 Economics Unit 4 examination. The content has been neither
approved nor endorsed by Edexcel and remains the sole responsibility of the
author.

Printed by MPG Books, Bodmin

Environmental information

The paper on which this title is printed is sourced from managed, sustainable
forests.

Contents

Introduction

■ ■ ■

Content Guidance

■ ■ ■

Questions and Answers

Introduction

Aims

This guide has been written to prepare students for Unit 4 of Edexcel's A-level (A2) GCE examinations in economics. It provides an overview of the knowledge and skills required to achieve a high grade in the examination for Industrial Economics. This unit looks at the price and output decisions of firms in a market economy and considers issues of market structure. An important focus of the specification for this unit is the role of government policy in supporting competitive markets. There are five main topics:

(1) The growth of firms: why and how firms might want to grow, the importance of entrepreneurship, vertical, horizontal and conglomerate integration, barriers to entry, internally financed growth, the importance of multinational firms, and measures of market concentration.

(2) Theory of the firm: an understanding of cost and revenue curves and profit maximisation, theories of perfect competition, monopolistic competition, oligopoly and monopoly, price discrimination, and the application of productive and allocative efficiency concepts to different market structures.

(3) Pricing and non-pricing strategies: the alternative objectives of firms, varieties of pricing strategy, non-price competition such as advertising and sales promotion, and the significance of collusion and cartels.

(4) Competition policy: the basic framework for competition policy in the UK and the EU, the impact of policy on both producers and consumers, and a consideration of the costs and benefits of competition policy.

(5) Regulation of privatised industries: the function of government regulators such as Ofgem and Oftel, RPI minus X price capping, and the effects of regulation on producers and consumers.

How to use this guide

This guide provides a summary of the knowledge and skills required for Unit 4. It also focuses on exam techniques, including typical questions and answers, and explains what the examiners are looking for. Common mistakes are highlighted and strategies for increasing marks are suggested. The guide should be used as a supplement to a taught course along with textbooks and other materials that teachers recommend.

This introduction explains the examination format and the skills that will be tested. It also provides useful tips on revision planning and sitting the examination. A 4-week revision programme for Unit 4 is also included.

The Content Guidance section provides an overview of the topics identifying what has to be learnt and explaining the theoretical requirements of the unit. There is an emphasis on the links *between* topics and the importance of the evaluation component at A2.

The final part of the guide provides questions and answers on the economic concepts and topics in Unit 4. There are three sets of ten supported multiple-choice questions, together with answers demonstrating how to go about maximising the score in these types of question.

Finally, there are three data–response questions covering the main topic areas, with a selection of student answers to give candidates an idea of the level of answer required to achieve a grade A. Some grade-C level answers are included to show what can go wrong under timed conditions. The answers include examiner's comments, which are a helpful way of getting to know the expectations of those who will mark the papers. After reviewing the Unit 4 topics, students should have a go at these sample questions, *ideally under timed conditions*, and then compare their work with the answers and comments provided. This will identify areas of weakness that require further work.

Exam format

Unit 4 makes up 30% of the total marks for the A2 (15% of the total A-level). It is worth a maximum of 90 Uniform Mark Scheme (UMS) marks. The exam has two sections. Section A is made up of ten compulsory supported multiple-choice questions. Section B has a choice of one from two data–response questions. Both sections are of equal worth, with a mark base of 40 per section, giving a maximum raw mark of 80.

As a rough guide to the standards required, the January 2002 examinations set the grade-A boundary at 49/80, grade C at 37/80 and grade E at 25/80. However, these grade thresholds change according to the examiner's perception of the quality of the candidates and the difficulty of the papers.

The amount of time allowed for the examination is 1 hour and 15 minutes. This leaves 35 minutes per section and 5 minutes for reading through the paper at the beginning and checking answers at the end. There is very little margin for error here — it is vital that candidates spend equal time on each section.

Assessment objectives

There are four assessment objectives, or sets of skills, in each unit of AS and A-level economics. When questions are set, these skills are very much in the examiner's mind. The objectives are *knowledge*, *application*, *analysis* and *evaluation* and are defined in the table overleaf. Notice that the evaluation component is much higher than at AS.

When questions are set, a great deal of thought is put into the choice of *command words*. These are the directive words in each question, such as define, explain and discuss. It is vital for candidates to understand the intention behind the command words because they signal different levels of expected response. As the questions at the end of this guide make clear, candidates can lose many marks if they disregard

Objective	Assessment objectives	A2 weighting
1	**Knowledge and understanding:** demonstrate knowledge and understanding of the specified content.	20%
2	**Application:** apply knowledge and critical understanding to problems and issues arising from both familiar and unfamiliar situations.	20%
3	**Analysis:** analyse economic problems and issues.	30%
4	**Evaluation:** evaluate economic arguments and evidence, making informed judgements.	30%

the command word. This is particularly true in the data–response section of Unit 4 where there are many evaluation marks to acquire.

Knowledge and understanding

The command words for this include: *define, outline* and *distinguish between*. For example, in Unit 4 candidates are expected to be able to define terms such as vertical integration, allocative efficiency and limit pricing. Candidates are also expected to understand the basic models of monopolistic competition, oligopoly and monopoly.

Application and analysis

These two assessment objectives are indicated by command words such as *analyse* and *explain*. Often the question will include instructions to draw a diagram. The idea here is for candidates to apply industrial economics to real-world case studies presented in the data–response. These are usually in the areas of the activities of major UK and multinational firms, competition policy and the regulation of privatised industries.

Evaluation

This is the assessment objective most often ignored by candidates. Command words include: *examine, evaluate, discuss, assess, comment upon* and *to what extent*. Any of these words in a question show that examiners expect candidates to demonstrate some critical understanding of the issues being discussed. Strategies for gaining evaluation marks include discussing the pros and cons of an argument and assessing the use of evidence presented in the passage.

Planning your revision: general points

Educational research shows unambiguously that you will remember your notes better if you learn them *more than once*. For this reason, you should survey the material for the entire unit well before you sit down to do final revision. For the June exam, start revising during the Easter holidays when you should:

- **Check that you have covered all elements of the specification.** This can be freely downloaded from the Edexcel website at **www.edexcel.org.uk**. The best version is in the 'Teachers' Guide' because it includes extended advice about the specification requirement. Your teachers should have provided you with past papers. If not, insist that they do so.

- **Get your notes in order.** Check that you have notes for each section of the specification. If you are in any doubt about which section (or unit) your notes should be filed under, consult your teachers as a matter of urgency.
- **Think about how you might be able to add value to your answers.** It pays to have some extra material at your command. For example, there is a wealth of information available on privatisation and competition policy on the internet. Further, the candidates who are certain to achieve grade A are those who have studied a relevant textbook *systematically* and not simply relied on lessons.
- **Do not cut out topics from your revision.** The Unit 4 question papers have ten compulsory questions drawn from the entire specification. It is not safe to ignore some topics because you are pressed for time. You must plan to cover the entire range of subjects. This is manageable if you allocate your time sensibly.
- **Begin to learn your notes systematically.** It is important that you adopt a method of committing your notes to memory. Merely reading them through whilst listening to music and drinking a cup of coffee is not going to get you very far — though, dangerously, it will *feel* like you have been revising. Everyone has a different method of learning things by heart, and as a *minimum* you must reduce your material to condensed lists of points. Your aim should be to get into a position where you can reproduce these lists by heart by the end of the Easter holiday. There is only one way that you can be sure that you have achieved this: testing yourself by writing out the lists having put the originals away.
- **Make use of your friends.** An excellent way of reinforcing learning is to discuss particular topics with friends. Try to teach a part of the specification to someone you know who is also taking the examination and get him or her to do the same for you.
- **Practise questions under timed conditions.** It is important to test yourself under pressure of time. If you have not done any timed work in school, make sure you are given the opportunity to do so. Use some of the questions at the back of this guide for extra practice.

A 4-week structured revision plan

For final revision in the weeks leading up to the examination, you should relearn the material, with an emphasis on trying to gain a complete knowledge of your notes. If you work efficiently this should not take very long — say half an hour a day for each unit. *It is better to do a small amount of revision every day than try to learn the whole course just before the exam.* If you have nine units to take, this would imply three hour-and-a-half sessions a day. It is unlikely that more intensive revision than this will be very productive.

Day	Week 1	Week 2	Week 3	Week 4
One	The birth and growth of firms. Small firms and their significance.	Productive and allocative efficiency.	Oligopoly theory, cartels and collusion.	Non-price competition, advertising, sales promotion.
Two	The motives for the growth of firms. Economies of scale.	Measures of market concentration. Barriers to entry.	Monopoly theory: diagrams, efficiency, profits.	Contestable markets.
Three	Internal and external growth. Types of integration.	Perfect competition theory.	Price discrimination.	Competition policy.
Four	Multinationals. Policy consequences of multinationals.	Monopolistic competition theory.	Cost-plus, predatory and limit pricing.	Regulation of privatised industries.
Five	Exam practice: do one set of multiple-choice questions from this guide.	Exam practice: do one set of multiple-choice questions from this guide.	Exam practice: data–response question from this guide.	Exam practice: data–response question from this guide.

How to answer supported multiple-choice questions

You will have had some experience of supported multiple-choice questions in Unit 1. In this unit, however, you have five answers to choose from and a total of ten questions. In Unit 4, 1 mark is awarded for the correct answer and a maximum of 3 marks for the explanation.

You can gain a maximum of 2 marks for explanation even if you have selected the wrong answer. It is therefore *always* worth writing something, however confused you are by the question. Just giving a definition of a key term included in the question is often worth a mark.

You can also gain a maximum of 2 marks for explaining why some of the alternatives are incorrect. This is a useful strategy too if you are not sure that your explanation of the correct alternative is detailed enough.

Further tips for the supported multiple-choice questions are:

- **Draw diagrams wherever possible.** These need to be clearly labelled and key areas or points indicated. It is often easier to explain an answer with a diagram, and diagrams should be at the forefront of your approach to these questions.
- **Use any diagrams provided.** If diagrams are included in the question, be sure to annotate them as part of your answer. For example, draw arrows showing the direction of movement implied by the question, or shade in a relevant area.
- **Be strict with your time allocation for each question.** All too often, candidates write at enormous length on the supported multiple-choice section and then cannot finish the data–response question.
- **Do not get stuck on a particular question.** Candidates often report that they were fazed by an unfamiliar expression or set of data. Don't waste time puzzling out

the unfamiliar, but instead write down some basic definitions and leave the question behind. If you have time, you can always come back to it at the end of the examination.

- **Pick up on the economic jargon terms in the question.** These will almost always be worth defining in your explanation.
- **Answer all the questions.** It is surprising that many candidates do not even guess the answers to questions they do not understand. There are no marks deducted for incorrect answers or explanations.
- **Practice really does make perfect.** The more multiple-choice questions you can find time to do before the exam the better. Your marks are likely to increase a great deal with practice. There are very few totally original multiple-choice questions on the theory of the firm and, if you do enough of them, you will begin to understand the logic behind how they are set.

A more general rule for supported multiple-choice questions is that you should look for the answer to the question *in the question* and not in the answers. That is, it often pays to try to answer the question before becoming distracted by the answers.

A final point: it is worth maintaining a (controlled) sense of paranoia as you do multiple-choice questions. Did that question say 'revenue maximisation' or 'profit maximisation'? Was there a 'not' in the middle of that question? Believe that your brain will play tricks on you in the exam. Check your answers and what you took to be the question carefully.

How to answer data–response questions

There is a choice between two data–response questions in Unit 4. Candidates should be well placed to answer either question and not waste time trying to decide which one to do. It is, however, worth checking through each question to make sure that there are no sections that you cannot answer. For example, if you have forgotten what contestability means, do not do a question that has 10 marks for a discussion of it.

The data–response questions for Unit 4 tend to come from three main areas: newspaper or magazine reports on the activities of firms; Competition Commission reports on mergers or other investigations; and articles on privatisation. It is therefore well worth getting into the habit of reading a broadsheet newspaper or *The Economist* magazine and asking yourself whether the articles would make good Unit 4 questions. It is worth visiting the Competition Commission website, **www.competition-commission.org.uk**, and studying some of the reports it has made available. There is also a wealth of material available on privatisation.

It is likely that each data–response question will include a mixture of text, graphics and data based on real companies. There are a number of basic rules to follow when trying to answer the questions:

- **Identify the economic theory behind the question.** Questions tend to be set with economic theory in mind. If at all possible, use the relevant theory rather than

writing a general answer. Do not hesitate to use theoretical diagrams and economic terms in your answer.

- **Answers should always be related to the context provided.** You need to apply the theory to the context. Purely theoretical answers are unlikely to score high marks. For example, a question asking about the extent to which price discrimination is possible in the railway industry demands more than a textbook list of the factors that enable price discrimination. What you need to do is list each factor and apply it to the railway industry. Talk about the same seat being priced differently according to the category of customer, the non-transferability of tickets etc.

- **Do not take key terms in the questions for granted.** Some strong candidates have a tendency to drop marks because they forget to include basic definitions. Be sure that you can define all the key terms in the Content Guidance section of this guide.

- **Make use of the text or data provided.** If the question says 'with reference to the passage', then you *must* use brief quotations from the passage to support your answer. Very often, the text will provide you with at least enough to make a good start to a question. On the other hand, do not reproduce large chunks of text from the passage because there is little point to answers that merely copy out large sections of the text provided.

- **Look carefully at the scale of graphs or bar charts.** The units of measurement matter — many candidates make mistakes in this area. Are the figures in thousands or millions? Or are they percentages?

- **Identify trends in data, not just levels.** If you are asked to describe data or are using them as evidence, then calculate percentage changes over the relevant time scale rather than just listing values.

- **Move beyond the confines of the data.** Unless the question specifically directs you to discuss only issues referred to in the data, you should widen the discussion as far as possible. Often, sections towards the end of each question allow a more general level of response. Use material from other case studies you have looked at and arguments or issues not included in the passage.

- **Be critical of the data provided.** The arguments put forward in the passage are not correct just because they appear in an examination paper. Every author makes a *selection* of evidence and arguments. It is always possible to put forward another point of view even if it is only a matter of different emphasis. There are marks available for candidates who demonstrate they are capable of achieving a degree of critical distance from the material provided.

- **Allocate time sensibly.** You have no more than about 45 minutes for the data–response question. Remember that it is much easier to score marks at the beginning of an answer than at the end. Do not spend so much time on the first few questions that you have to leave the last questions blank. Also, be sensible about spending time on each section: 2-mark questions require much shorter answers than 10-mark questions.

- **Keep up to date.** Industrial economics is a changing field. For example, the basic framework of competition policy changes over time as the Competition Commission makes new judgements or as governments come and go. The record of privatised industries becomes clearer with hindsight, e.g. the performance of Railtrack.

- **Pay particular attention to key words.** One of the problems of doing a data–response question in timed conditions is that the key words change with each question. One moment you are writing elementary definitions and the next some critical evaluation is required. It is vital that you keep up with these shifts of expectation. Some examples include:

    Define — make clear the meaning of a term. You should make a list of all the terms in the specification and commit the definitions to memory. It is often worth providing an illustrative example to back up a definition.

    Analyse — explain the economic logic behind a situation. Often the use of a diagram is helpful here.

    Using diagrams — these need to be presented clearly. Many candidates draw their diagrams too small — a third of a side is not unreasonable. Label the axes. If you have equilibrium points to indicate, dot down or across to the axes and label these values. If your diagram is showing a move from one equilibrium to another, draw arrows along the axes to show the changes. If your diagram goes wrong, put a single line through it and start again. Under no circumstances should you submit a diagram with some of the lines on it crossed out.

    Examine, evaluate, discuss, assess, to what extent — these are evaluation key words directing candidates to examine critically the matter at hand. A good strategy is to rehearse the pros and cons of the arguments concerned. You should appraise the balance of argument and indicate which points have the greatest or least significance. For evaluation sections with a high number of marks, you should come to a conclusion at the end of your answer.

Grade descriptions

Edexcel provides official grade descriptions for examiners to use as a guide to their marking. The grade you achieve will depend on the extent to which you have met the four assessment objectives described above. However, you do not have to give perfect answers to achieve a grade A. The examiners are very much aware that you are under considerable time pressure when you do these units and Unit 4 is no exception. There is a great deal to do and there is no way that you will be able to cover every aspect of a question during the exam.

Do not panic if you know you have got part of a question wrong, because it is still possible to achieve a high grade. Shortcomings in some aspects of your examination answers may be balanced by better performance elsewhere.

The author's comments are in italics after the official grade descriptions listed below.

Grade A

Candidates will demonstrate in-depth knowledge and critical understanding of a wide range of economic theories and concepts. They will apply this knowledge and understanding to analyse familiar and unfamiliar situations, issues and problems using appropriate numerical and non-numerical techniques accurately. They will evaluate evidence and arguments effectively, making reasoned judgements to present appropriate and well-supported conclusions.

In practice, two things distinguish grade-A candidates. The first is a thorough knowledge of the basic specification so that there are few, if any, blank sections in their answers. The second is an ability to evaluate — the last line of the official description is the most important.

Grade C

Candidates will demonstrate knowledge and understanding of a limited range of economic theories and concepts. They will show some ability to use this knowledge and understanding in order to analyse familiar and unfamiliar situations, issues and problems making use of numerical and non-numerical techniques. Candidates' evaluation of evidence and arguments will be limited.

Grade-C candidates tend to have a good basic knowledge of only some parts of the specification. They tend to leave some sections unanswered and to make only limited use of the data and passage provided. They pay very little attention to the meaning of key words and tend to ignore commands to evaluate.

It is worth observing that the easiest grade to target is grade A. Because of the way the Uniform Mark Scheme operates, it is by no means out of the question to emerge with 100% UMS with considerably less than this on the raw mark base.

Content
Guidance

Industrial economics consists of both theory and applied topics. The traditional and intellectually rigorous **theory of the firm** is an essential grounding in how economists think about industry and the interaction of firms and markets. It forms the basis for an applied study of competition policy and the regulation of privatised industries.

The Content Guidance section focuses on essential information, including economic concepts and models that students need to understand for Unit 4: Industrial Economics. These are explained under the following headings:

Introduction to industrial economics

Background from Units 1 and 2

Industrial economics looks at the reasons for the growth of firms, their tendency to merge with other firms, and the logic behind their price and output decisions. Before starting the main theory, there are a number of concepts from Unit 1 and Unit 2 that need to be incorporated into Unit 4 studies. These are covered in this introductory section.

The birth and growth of firms

Firms begin from the activities of *entrepreneurs* who take the *risk* of bringing together other factors of production: land, labour and capital. There are a number of constraints to this process, the most important of which is finance. Many potentially successful firms fail because they are unable to generate cash flow early enough and have insufficient resources to fall back on. Other significant factors include the tax incentives on offer for people to start businesses — whether tax on profits is less than tax on income, for example — and the willingness of banks to risk lending to new firms.

Motives for the growth of firms

A number of factors explain why a firm may want to grow in size. The first set of reasons concerns the *economies of scale* that occur when a firm experiences falling long-run average costs as it expands. The main factors are:

- A larger output may justify the use of assembly-line technology allowing rapid falls in average costs.
- The firm may be able to overcome indivisibilities of machinery. If the firm has two processes — one where machines operate at five units an hour and another where machines operate at seven units an hour — it will need to raise output to 35 units an hour before all the machines are operating at full capacity.
- As the firm's size increases, it will be able to have a more thoroughgoing division of labour. Specialised workers (managers, accountants, sales representatives) may be more efficient than individuals trying to perform multiple tasks.
- There may be volume economies in production. A firm doubling the dimensions of its warehouses, pipelines or lorries will more than double its usable space.
- There may be pecuniary economies from bulk buying. This is not confined to purchases of raw materials but extends to borrowing money, advertising and transport costs.
- The firm will be able to finance research and development into new products and technologies.

A further set of reasons for the growth of firms involves the motivation of the owners or directors:

- As the firm grows it will gain a larger market share and this may give it a degree of market power and more influence on the market price. The result is likely to be higher profits.
- Large firms tend to pay their managers higher salaries than small firms.
- Some entrepreneurs are motivated by the idea of growth and the ambition to run the largest and most successful firm of its type in the country, or beyond.
- A successful record of growth is often a qualification for directors to move jobs to larger, more prestigious companies.

Internal growth

As a firm increases in size, it may follow the route of *internal expansion*:
- Larger firms accumulate assets that are more valuable and these can serve as collateral for loans to finance further expansion.
- Profits may be ploughed back into investment to increase capacity.
- Only large firms will be able to afford a stock-market listing. Raising money in this way can be a lot cheaper than borrowing from banks.

External growth

Mergers occur when two companies agree to form a single firm. Acquisitions occur when one company buys up the shares of another, sometimes against the wishes of the target company's board of directors.

External growth takes three main forms:
- **Horizontal integration** takes place when a company merges with or acquires another company at the same stage of production as itself. An example is the purchase of one airline by another. Horizontal integration is likely to realise economies of scale through rationalisation of management, synergies in research and development and as an opportunity to shed surplus labour. Market power can also be achieved because the resulting firm will have a greater market share.
- **Vertical integration** occurs when a company buys another at an earlier or later stage of production than itself. An ice-cream maker purchasing a dairy farm is an example of *backward* vertical integration. If the firm buys a chain of retail outlets to sell its ice cream, this would be *forward* vertical integration. Benefits of vertical integration include overcoming asymmetries of information (e.g. finding out the true costs of producing ice cream) and the elimination of third-party profit margins. With forward vertical integration, market power can also be achieved because the firm can exclude others from its newly acquired retail outlets by stocking only its own ice cream.
- **Conglomerate integration** takes place when a firm merges with or acquires another company in an unrelated industry and this could be something as unlikely as a water company acquiring a football club. The main purpose of conglomerate integration is to allow the firm to diversify against risk. Having operations in different sectors of the economy protects the firm from a downturn in one of them.

Multinational companies

Multinational companies (MNCs) play an important role in the UK economy. Foreign direct investment from MNCs is likely to have significant regional multiplier effects as people gain employment, sometimes at higher wages than paid by UK firms. Foreign firms often introduce world-class management techniques and access to the latest technology. The exports of multinationals contribute to foreign exchange earnings, and there are likely to be gains to other firms from improved infrastructure. The government gains corporation tax revenue from an MNC's UK profits.

There are, however, disadvantages to multinational involvement in a national economy. MNCs may require large government subsidies to persuade them to locate in a particular country, but can be footloose and move in pursuit of subsidies offered by other countries. If a country's macroeconomic position looks uncertain, MNCs may make their excuses and leave.

Efficiency concepts

When assessing the performance of firms, it is useful to make reference to the following efficiency concepts:

- **Productive efficiency** occurs when a firm operates at the lowest point of its average cost curve. Output is therefore achieved with the least possible resource cost per unit.
- **Allocative efficiency** occurs when a firm sets a price equal to marginal cost. This ensures that scarce resources are allocated to where they are most valued by consumers.
- **X inefficiency** describes the bureaucracy and complacency — and hence the higher costs — of a firm with too much market power.

Basic cost concepts

There are several kinds of costs:

- **Fixed costs** are those that are independent of output, e.g. rent on land.
- **Variable costs** are those that change directly with output, e.g. the fuel costs of running a production line.
- **Average costs** are the cost per unit of output.
- **Marginal costs** are the cost of an *additional* unit of output.

Measures of market concentration

The specification requires candidates to know the measure of market concentration. This measures the percentage share of the largest *n* firms in the industry of some important market characteristic. For example, the 'five-firm concentration ratio by sales' measures the market share of the largest five firms in the industry. Concentration ratios can also be calculated for employment. An industry with a high concentration ratio is said to be *highly concentrated*.

Examination skills and concepts

- Listing economies of scale applied to a particular industry.
- Understanding how the stock market acts as a source of finance for firms wishing to expand.
- Distinguishing between the three main kinds of integration and explaining reasons for each.

- Explaining why MNCs are an important part of UK industry. Are there any risks to an economy with a large element of inward direct investment?
- Understanding the concept of market power and its likely effect on consumers.

Common examination errors

- Confusing falling average costs with falling costs. Remember that the *total* costs of a firm benefiting from economies of scale are *rising*.
- Being vague about the kinds of economy of scale that might be achieved: try to identify some of these.
- In the data–response questions, it is important to relate concepts to the particular industry referred to in the data. General answers, or ones that merely repeat theory, are unlikely to score high marks.
- Thinking that a 'more concentrated' industry means a larger number of firms. Be sure to understand that, in fact, a greater degree of industrial concentration implies a *smaller* number of firms.

Useful exercises

- Read the financial pages of a broadsheet newspaper and look out for stories of firms merging. To what extent does the list of factors above explain why the firms merged?
- Use the internet to collect data on the relative importance of small firms to the UK economy.
- Visit the Treasury website at **www.hm-treasury.gov.uk**. What help does the government currently offer small firms?
- Collect case studies of MNCs that have recently started or stopped producing in the UK. What factors seemed to have influenced their choice?
- Revise ideas from Unit 2 and discuss with a fellow student why firms exist. A good start is to ask why a school is not just a collection of independently contracted teachers. Why do schools pay all teachers the same salary scale? There is a national shortage of economics teachers and a surplus of history teachers: why are economics teachers not paid more? What does this suggest about the nature of firms?

Linkages and common themes

Economics is a fairly strongly integrated body of knowledge, so do not think of Unit 4 as separate from the rest of the course. The following linkages to other units should be thought through:

- The existence and shape of supply curves is an important aspect of this module. Unit 4 identifies the conventional upward-sloping supply curve of Unit 1 as a special case that holds only for perfect competition and shows that monopolies do not have supply curves at all.
- A major reason why firms exist and have a motive to integrate is information failure. This links to the Unit 2 way of viewing firms as institutions designed to deal with market failure. Suppose some pupils set up in business at school. Why might they want to appoint someone to act as manager of the new firm?
- The role of multinationals will recur in both Unit 5B (Development Economics) and Unit 6 as part of globalisation studies. Be sure to acquire case studies of MNC investment in the UK.

Theory of the firm

Theory and application

This section provides an overview of the theory of the firm required by the Unit 4 specification. While the emphasis should be on the application of theoretical concepts to real examples, candidates should be able to draw the diagrams presented below and use them to analyse shocks to the market. Candidates should also be able to compare market structures in terms of pricing, profitability and efficiency.

Perfect competition

The model of perfect competition makes several assumptions about market structure, and these assumptions have implications for the conduct and performance of firms. The model assumes:

- **Many buyers and sellers** with no individual agent having overall market power.
- **Homogeneous goods** whereby firms sell the same product without branding or advertising.
- **Perfect information** with consumers always knowing where the good is on offer at the lowest price.
- **Profit maximisation** where pursuit of maximum profit is what motivates firms.
- **Freedom of entry and exit** with no barriers to entry and the ability for firms to leave the industry without cost.

These assumptions ensure that firms are price takers. This means that no firm will be able to raise its price above that of its rivals, because consumers will immediately switch supplier. The perfect competition model results in *long-run equilibrium* between firms and industry, as illustrated in the following graph:

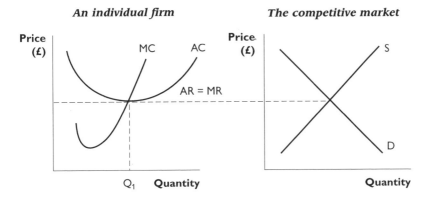

There are a number of aspects of this diagram that students should understand:
- **Always draw a diagram representing a firm alongside one for the market.** In perfect competition, it makes little sense to draw firms by themselves because they take the price from the market. Therefore, initially read the above diagram

from right to left. The equilibrium price is determined in the market, and this then determines the average revenue for the firm — the firm is small enough to be able to sell as much of the product as it likes at this price.

- **AR = MR.** If the revenue per unit is constant, then the revenue from selling one extra unit must be equal to the average. Otherwise, the average would change.
- **The relationship between the firm's average costs and marginal costs.** Recall that average costs are the cost *per unit* of output and that marginal costs are the costs of an *extra* unit of output. For average cost to be falling, the marginal must be below the average. Only when marginal rises above average cost does the latter start to rise. It is therefore important that in a diagram of firms in any market structure the curve MC must cut AC at its minimum point.
- **The firm will profit maximise at Q_1.** To profit maximise, the firm must set MR = MC. If the firm produces an extra unit beyond Q_1, then MC would be greater than MR, i.e. that extra unit would add more to cost than to revenue, and profits would fall.
- **An increase in demand would leave the price and output of the firm unchanged in the long run.** A rise in demand would raise the equilibrium market price. The firm would increase output to where MC is equal to the higher MR and make supernormal profits. Because there are assumed to be no barriers to entry, new firms will be attracted into the market and the supply curve will shift to the right. This reduces the market equilibrium price until each firm is once again making only normal profit. You should be able to illustrate this process on the diagram.
- **The firm will be allocatively efficient in both the short and long run.** Since the firm is a price taker, P = AR = MR. Profit maximising implies MR = MC. Therefore P = MC.
- **The firm will be productively efficient in the long run.** The forces at work in the market described above ensure that the firm is always returned to the minimum of its average cost curve.
- **The firm will make only normal profit in the long run.** New entrants drive the price down to the minimum level necessary to keep entrepreneurs in the industry.

The model of perfect competition makes strong assumptions about the amount of information available and the absence of sunk costs facing new entrants. In the market for manufactured goods, products are never completely homogeneous — factors such as packaging create differentiations.

Monopolistic competition

This model has the same assumptions as perfect competition, except that a firm's products are differentiated from its rivals. Monopolistic competition does not refer to monopoly because many buyers and sellers are assumed and — by giving its product different characteristics — each firm creates a certain amount of brand loyalty. Differentiated products mean that firms do not operate as price takers. Therefore, each one can charge a slightly different price from its competitors whilst keeping most of its customers.

The diagram below shows a firm in monopolistic competition in long-run equilibrium:

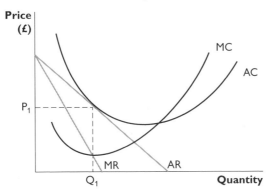

Long-run equilibrium in monopolistic competition

The key aspects of analysing models of monopolistic competition include:

- **Check the intersections on the diagram.** MC must cross the minimum of AC. The profit-maximising firm produces at Q_1 where MR – MC. The equilibrium price is at P_1.
- **MR is below AR.** The firm faces a downward-sloping demand curve, AR. For the average to fall, marginal revenue must be below the average. In fact, MR will be twice as steep as AR. Notice that AR = MR only for the *first* unit of output: the curves should join on the price axis.
- **The firm makes only normal profit in the long run.** Because there is freedom of entry, new firms will be attracted in by any supernormal profit and the demand curve faced by existing firms will fall until it is tangent to the AC curve where the firm is making normal profit.
- **The firm is neither allocatively nor productively efficient.** The diagram shows that price is greater than marginal cost and that the firm is producing at above the minimum of its average cost. Each firm is therefore said to have *excess capacity*. Notice how a small change in the assumptions of perfect competition destroys the efficiency results of that model.
- **In the short run, an increase in demand will cause the firm to raise output and make supernormal profit.** Remember that if AR shifts, MR must shift too, and so the point where MR = MC will move to the right.
- **In the long run, demand will become more elastic.** As new firms enter the market, they will introduce products with new characteristics. This increases the number of substitutes available for consumers. The demand faced by incumbent firms will become more elastic as it falls back to a new tangency with AC. The firm's long-run output will therefore *increase* following the increase in demand.

Evaluation

In evaluating the model of monopolistic competition, note the tension between the assumption of product differentiation and freedom of entry and exit. It is also not particularly clear in this model how long-run equilibrium will be achieved: as new firms enter the industry, their products will be nearer in characteristics to some of the incumbents than to others. Some firms could go out of business whilst others are still making supernormal profit.

Monopoly

A monopoly is a sole supplier. However, the government defines a firm as potentially having market power with as little as 25% market share. There are various kinds of monopoly:

- A **natural monopoly** occurs in industries with economies of scale at all marketable levels of output. For example, it would make little sense to have competing water suppliers all laying their own pipelines. Candidates are expected to be able to draw a natural monopoly diagram showing that high sunk costs make both AC and MC fall with output:

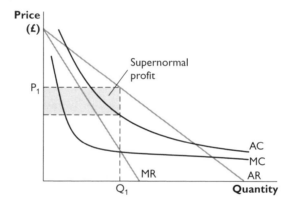

A profit-maximising natural monopoly

- A **local monopoly** occurs when there is no practical alternative to using the available supplier, e.g. using the cafeteria in a sports centre.
- A **legal monopoly** is one protected by law. For example, it is still illegal for firms other than the Post Office to deliver letters for less than £1.
- A **competitive monopoly** occurs when power accrues through merger or acquisition.

Barriers to entry

Monopolies often maintain their position through barriers to entry, including:

- **Legal protection** via patents, copyrights and trademarks.
- **Advertising** with the effect of raising sunk costs and therefore also raising the risks of entry into the industry.
- **Limit pricing** where a firm reduces price below a new entrant's average costs, thus ensuring potential rivals know they would make a loss were they to come into the market. The incumbent firm may well have greater financial reserves than the new entrant, and when the threat has passed, the firm can raise prices back to profit-maximising levels.

content guidance

● **Research and development expenditure** to keep products technologically up to date and make it more expensive for new entrants to succeed. Notice that this barrier may act in the interests of consumers.

The diagram below shows a profit-maximising monopoly:

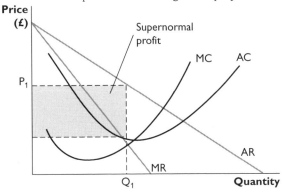

A profit-maximising monopolist

There are a number of points to note about a profit-maximising monopolist:
● As in previous theory of the firm diagrams, profits are maximised where MR = MC.
● There is no reason why a monopoly should necessarily make supernormal profits. If demand for its product falls or its costs increase, a firm may make a loss.
● The firm can set price or output but not both. Having set a profit-maximising level of output, the price will be determined by the demand curve.
● Monopolies are productively inefficient and there is no reason why the profit-maximising level of output should coincide with minimum average costs.
● Monopolies are also allocatively inefficient. They have an incentive to drive up prices above marginal costs in order to increase their profits.
● An increase in demand will raise the firm's output and profit. However, barriers to entry will allow the firm to continue to earn supernormal profit into the long run.

Price discrimination

Price discrimination takes place when a firm charges different customers different prices for the same product. The conditions for successful price discrimination are:
● Monopoly power sufficient to avoid being undercut by rival companies.
● The ability to prevent second-hand resale of the product and to prevent the undermining of sales at higher prices.
● The possibility of identifying different groups of customers with different price elasticities of demand.

In the diagram overleaf, the firm has divided its market into two groups of customers. The first one has inelastic demand and the second has elastic demand. The firm's marginal revenue curve will be the horizontal summation of the two market MR curves and this results in the kink illustrated in the firm's diagram. The firm then sets MR = MC to profit maximise, which in turn determines the price to be set in each market.

The lower the elasticity of demand, the higher is the profit-maximising price.

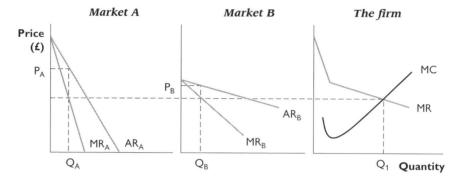

A useful way to think of price discrimination is as a firm's attempt to capture consumer surplus. As such it appears, at first sight, to operate against the interests of consumers. However, some low-income consumers may gain from price discrimination because they can purchase the product at a lower price. An example is senior citizens' rail cards.

Oligopoly

If a few large *interdependent* firms dominate a market, this market is defined as oligopolistic. Such markets have high concentration ratios. Firms second-guessing each other's price and output decisions can lead to market instability and, in reaction, some form of collusion sometimes occurs. This can have adverse effects on consumers. There are three main forms of collusion in oligopoly theory:

- **Cartels** comprise firms making formal agreements to fix price or output. OPEC is a good example, with the countries involved meeting regularly to fix output quotas in order to influence the world oil price.
- **Secret collusion** occurs in countries such as the UK where cartels are illegal. Many companies have been caught trying to fix prices, e.g. in the cement industry.
- **Tacit collusion** is where firms act *as if* they have made an agreement, even though they have not discussed the matter. An important form of tacit collusion is price *leadership* where firms imitate the behaviour of the dominant firm in the industry.

The complexity of oligopoly theory means there is no single diagram to represent it and different teachers adopt different approaches. Candidates do not have to draw the complicated kinked demand curve, though this would be perfectly acceptable to the examiners.

The consequences of firms' interdependence are forms of collusion likely to lead to price fixing and exploitation of consumers. When firms are reluctant to compete on price, *non-price competition* has them competing through variations in packaging, special offers and reward points. Nonetheless, price wars are likely from time to time and they sometimes reach extravagant lengths, such as holiday companies giving away holidays.

Cartels (either overt or covert) are illegal under UK competition policy. The 1998 Competition Act allows the Office of Fair Trading (OFT) to fine firms operating cartels up to 10% of turnover for each year the cartel has been in operation (up to a maximum of 3 years). The European Union (EU) has similar powers for firms that span national borders.

Examination skills and concepts

- Distinguishing between the four main market structures of perfect competition, monopolistic competition, oligopoly and monopoly.
- Being clear about the efficiency results for each market structure and remembering that only perfect competition achieves both allocative and productive efficiency.
- Going beyond statements that profit maximisation is where MR = MC to examine what happens to profit *at the margin* as output is increased beyond this point.
- Fitting theoretical models to real-life industries. For example, Unilever and Procter & Gamble dominate the automatic washing machine soap powder market. This soap market is thus oligopolistic and has a high market concentration ratio with inter-dependence of decision-making. The situation of sterling in foreign-exchange markets is much closer to perfect competition because sterling is homogeneous, there is perfect information and there are many buyers and sellers (though there may be some entry costs).

Common examination errors

- Confusing monopolistic competition with monopoly. Remember that the former concerns markets where there are *many* buyers and sellers.
- Being unable to draw the main diagrams accurately. Pay particular attention to the long-run equilibrium diagram for monopolistic competition because candidates seem to find this very difficult to draw under timed conditions. Start by drawing the AR and MR curves, then put in an AC tangent to AR and finally make sure the MC curve cuts the MR curve vertically below the point of tangency.
- Marking the price set by a monopoly across from where MR = MC, rather than from the demand curve.

Useful exercises

- Draw diagrams illustrating the effect of an increase in demand for a product for firms in perfect competition, monopolistic competition and monopoly. Compare the resulting changes in price, output and profit. *Hint*: always start such an analysis in long-run equilibrium.
- Repeat the exercise above, but this time for a fall in demand.
- Draw a diagram of a monopoly making a loss in the short run. Indicate on the diagram the loss-making area.

Linkages and common themes

- The theories of monopoly, monopolistic competition and perfect competition assume profit-maximising behaviour and similar cost curves for each market structure.
- An initial understanding of the average to marginal relationship can then be applied to costs, revenues and profits.

A useful way to summarise this section is shown on the following table.

Market structure	Number of firms	Market concentration	Long-run efficiency	Long-run profits
Perfect competition	Very many	Very low	Allocative, technical	Normal
Monopolistic competition	Very many	Very low	Neither	Normal
Oligopoly	A few	High	Neither	Supernormal
Monopoly	One	Very high	Neither	Supernormal

Alternative strategies for the firm

Alternative objectives

The traditional theory of the firm outlined above ignores the fact that, in certain circumstances, the owners or directors of a company may adopt different objectives. These are covered under the headings below.

Profit maximisation

This seems to be a good approximation to the activities of many individually run companies. Firms produce where MR = MC.

Revenue maximisation

In large public limited companies (PLCs), there is a divorce between ownership and control. The shareholders may only meet once a year at the company's annual general meeting (AGM) and it is essential for them to appoint a board of directors as agents to manage the company on their behalf. The directors, whilst aiming to satisfy the shareholders sufficiently to keep their jobs, may have rather different objectives than profit maximisation. By maximising revenue rather than profit, the directors may be able to generate extra expenditure on perks for themselves such as bigger company cars and headquarters that are more prestigious. To maximise revenue, the firm will produce where MR = 0.

Sales maximisation

This is defined as the maximum level of output that can be produced without making a loss. To achieve this, a firm needs to produce up to the point where AR = AC. The motives for such an objective might be an attempt to increase market share (whilst still making normal profit) or as a strategy of deterring the entry of rival firms which may have higher average costs. At the incumbent firm's sales-maximising price, the new entrants will therefore be forced into making losses.

Satisficing behaviour

Often, the information required to make maximising decisions of the kind described above is unavailable, or too costly to acquire. This is particularly true of the precise position of the demand curve faced by the firm. The firm may find it more rational to adopt rules of thumb (e.g. price mark-up strategies) than to determine maximising levels of output.

Pricing strategies

A firm may adopt a variety of pricing strategies according to its position in the market. Firms in perfect competition have no choice other than to accept the prevailing market equilibrium price. However, all other firms have some flexibility in the ways they may adopt to further short- or long-term goals.

Cost–plus pricing

This is where a firm charges a price based on average costs plus a percentage profit mark-up. This may be due to uncertainty about demand combined with knowledge that average costs are fairly constant. The fixed mark-up then ensures that the firm will make a satisfactory, if not maximising, level of profit.

Predatory pricing

A price set deliberately below average cost in order to make a loss in the short run and thus drive rival firms out of the industry. Prices can then be raised to maximise profits in the long run.

Limit pricing

This form of pricing is used to prevent new firms coming in to the industry. It is likely that existing firms enjoy the economies of scale to reduce prices to just above average costs and thus guarantee that any smaller scale new entrant would make a loss. When the threat of new entry has passed, the firm can raise its prices back to profit-maximising levels.

Non-pricing strategies

Firms may use a variety of non-price strategies to preserve or increase their market share.

Advertising

Many large firms — even those with monopoly levels of market share — have large advertising budgets. This can have a number of advantageous effects for the firm. First, the resulting brand loyalty reduces the price elasticity of demand and allows the firm to raise price and profit. Second, the expenditure represents a potential sunk cost to prospective new entrants which are made to realise that they too would need to advertise extensively were they to join the market.

Sales promotion policies

The firm may use packaging to great effect to promote product image. This can be combined with the fruits of research and development expenditure as the product is developed — hence the number of basic household goods with 'New!' labels on them. The firm may use a number of other promotion policies including competitions and free gifts.

Examination skills and concepts

- Illustrating the different objectives of firms diagrammatically, e.g. to distinguish between profit-maximising and revenue-maximising levels of output.
- Applying concepts of price and non-price competition to a case-study firm, e.g. choosing a product — such as powder for automatic washing machines — and studying the way it is promoted.

Common examination errors

- Confusing sales maximisation with revenue maximisation, possibly because some textbooks refer to 'sales revenue maximisation'. For this unit, rely on the terminology used above.
- Confusing predatory and limit pricing. The former seeks to eliminate existing firms, the latter to prevent the entry of *new* firms.

Useful exercises

- Draw a standard monopoly diagram and mark on the output levels where a firm is profit maximising, revenue maximising, allocatively efficient, productively efficient and sales maximising.
- Think of ways in which the concept of satisficing behaviour could be extended more generally in economic analysis. Herbert Simon developed the concept — search the internet for examples of how his ideas have been applied.

Linkages and common themes

The idea behind this section of the specification is to move understanding beyond the traditional theory of the firm. One way of integrating the new material is to think about the difference between short-run and long-run profit maximisation. There is little point in a firm maintaining a high price in the short term if its market would then be competed away. It makes sense to adopt alternative *short-run* strategies if this contributes to greater market power in the long run.

Contestability and competition policy

Contestable markets

The concept of contestability is an important part of the Unit 4 specification. Unfortunately the idea is not always well covered in textbooks and — judging from exam scripts — some students have not been taught the relevant ideas. In fact, the central concept is quite easy to understand and to apply to particular industries. It plays a major role when the Competition Commission decides whether to allow a merger to take place.

There is a contestable market where there is a credible threat of new entry to that market. For this to be the case, potential new entrants need to access the latest production techniques so as to be able to compete at similar levels of cost. Crucially, they also need to be able to leave the industry without excessive exit costs — otherwise they will be disinclined to take the *risk* of entry.

The key idea involved in the theory of contestable markets is therefore that of *sunk costs* that are not recoupable should a firm decide to leave its industry. The presence of high sunk costs can lead to an unwillingness of entrepreneurs to enter the industry. Examples of factors affecting the level of contestability include:

- **The reputation of the firm** where potential entrants may fear that the incumbent firm will adopt ruthless pricing or non-pricing strategies.
- **Investment costs** in specialised equipment that may be difficult to sell second hand. Even if the new firm's investments can be sold on, they will often lose value (depreciate) soon after being purchased. This is particularly true in markets where there is rapid technological change, e.g. internet-based industries.
- **The level of advertising** where incumbent firms with well-known brands can only be rivalled with high levels of advertising. This is a sunk cost.
- **Natural monopoly** elements to the industry, such as the supply of water to residential homes in London, are unlikely to be highly contestable.
- **Information asymmetry** where the incumbent firm has know-how that is unavailable to the potential entrant. This raises entry costs substantially.

The idea behind the theory of contestable markets is that competitiveness does not depend on market structure. Even a monopoly may operate in a contestable market. The *threat* of new entry will be enough to ensure that the monopoly makes only normal profit and acts *as if* it is in a competitive situation. The threat of hit-and-run tactics — where new firms come in to grab any supernormal profits and then leave freely because there are no sunk costs — should be sufficient to ensure that the monopoly acts efficiently.

It should therefore be clear why the concept of contestability is important to the competition authorities. A merger taking place in an industry with high sunk costs is likely to be of much greater concern than one in a contestable market — cartel-like behaviour and the exercise of market power against the interests of consumers are likely to occur.

Evaluating the theory of contestable markets raises a number of issues:
- No industries are perfectly contestable or completely lacking in contestability. It is always a question of degree.
- It is difficult to observe the implications of contestability directly. Its predicted effects revolve around the threat of new entry, and this may be in the mind of the incumbent.
- Finding out the cost structures of incumbent firms is difficult because the information is commercially sensitive. Therefore, it is often difficult to judge whether the firm is pricing at competitive levels or not.

Competition policy 1: mergers

The 1973 Fair Trading Act is the foundation of UK competition policy. Any merger or acquisition involving more than 25% market share in the UK or which involves the targeting of more than £70 million of worldwide assets is *eligible for referral* to the Competition Commission.

The Commission has only one thing to establish in its investigation, which is whether a proposed merger or acquisition is in the *public interest*. It has the power to impose conditions on the merger going ahead — that part of the company must be sold off, for example — or to recommend that the merger be allowed or prohibited. The final decision rests with the Secretary of State for Trade and Industry.

Public interest covers the following issues:
- Whether consumers will gain or lose from the proposed merger. For example, higher prices would result in a reduction in consumer surplus.
- Will new products be more or less likely after the merger? This is the question of consumer choice.
- Will there be adverse employment consequences from the merger? This may be particularly true if the companies involved are major employers in their regions.
- To what extent will the merger allow the company to be more competitive in world markets through, for example, economies of scale?

An assessment of UK mergers policy raises a number of questions:
- Is the policy consistent over time? A problem of the current regime is that the final decision lies with the Secretary of State and this introduces a degree of political arbitrariness.
- Is the framework transparent? That is, can companies contemplating a merger assess the rules under which the merger will be judged?
- To what extent is there an overlap between UK and EU competition policy?
- Is the policy framework tough enough/too tough?

These issues are best addressed by looking at some case studies of companies investigated by the Commission.

Competition policy 2: monopoly policy

An important change in UK competition policy took place with the 1998 Competition Act. This greatly strengthened the powers of the Office of Fair Trading (OFT) to investigate companies suspected of abusing a monopoly position. The OFT must first determine whether a firm has a *dominant* market position, and has interpreted this to mean a local or national market share of more than 40%. It then investigates whether the firm is exploiting this position by unfair pricing or other restrictive practices.

The OFT has considerable powers. It can raid the offices of firms thought to be colluding to look for incriminating evidence. Fines of up to 10% of annual turnover for each year of the offence can be imposed (up to a maximum of 3 years).

Examination skills and concepts

- Applying the concept of contestability to a case study presented as part of the data–response section and thinking through the likely sunk costs. It is also important to be able to evaluate the degree of contestability in an industry.
- Evaluating the public interest issues of a merger case study. Prepare a list of public interest issues and think through each one for a sample merger or acquisition.
- Making a limited evaluation of UK competition policy. The government is currently drafting legislation to change the framework of policy. Why might this be thought to be necessary? For clues on this question, visit the Department of Trade and Industry's website at **www.dti.gov.uk**.

Common examination errors

- Confusing the idea of contestability with barriers to entry. It is important when discussing contestability to talk explicitly about the likely sunk costs for the firm.
- Being vague about the context of UK competition policy. Although candidates are *not* required to know details about legislation, they should be able to distinguish between the work of the Competition Commission and the Office of Fair Trading. Students should understand the difference between merger investigations and enquiries into market dominance. Some idea of the problems of UK merger control in an EU context is also required.
- Being unsure about the 25% threshold for investigation by the Competition Commission.

Useful exercises

- Make a list of the sunk costs that would be incurred by a firm that wanted to set up a rival automatic washing machine powder to those produced by Unilever and Procter & Gamble. Which costs could the firm recoup?
- Discuss with a friend taking the A-level course whether the concept of contestability undermines the traditional theory of the firm. Does the theory itself have any weaknesses?

- Visit the Competition Commission's website and download the summary of two of its recent merger reports. How do these reports suggest the Commission judges the question of the public interest? The address of the site is www.competition-commission.uk.

Linkages and common themes

The aim of this section has been to move from theory to the applied side of industrial economics. Students are not expected to know a great deal of institutional or legal detail, but are expected to understand the broad framework of UK competition policy. The way policy relates to theoretical issues discussed in the 'Theory of the firm' section is important — in particular the likely effects of mergers on price, output and profit. This then leads on naturally to a discussion of productive and allocative efficiency issues.

Regulation of privatised industries

Recent history

The Thatcher government of the 1980s introduced a policy of thoroughgoing privatisation of state-run industries. British Telecom, British Airways, the rail industry, gas, electricity and the water industry were all transferred to private ownership. Unfortunately — though perhaps inevitably — many of these companies ended up as regional or national monopolies. The government therefore introduced a system of *regulation* to control the activities of the new companies.

RPI minus X regulation

The main method of regulating the privatised industries in the UK is *price capping*, with the government appointing an independent regulator to monitor the activities of each privatised company and to set the prices. Prices are set with a formula based on the retail price index (RPI).

The RPI minus X price cap has the regulator assessing the efficiency gains it thinks a firm can reasonably achieve: this determines a value for X. For example, a cap of RPI minus 4% means that the firm is allowed to raise its prices each year by no more than the rate of inflation *less* 4%. So, if inflation is 2.5%, then the firm will have to *reduce* its prices by 1.5%.

Many privatised firms were created as private sector monopolies. The fear was that these firms would exploit their market power and drive up prices. The regulator therefore uses price capping as a surrogate for competition, and attempts to force through efficiency improvements that would have been made in the presence of rival firms.

A major advantage of price capping is the incentive it creates for firms to cut costs by more than the value of X. The firm can keep all the profits it makes by these efficiency gains.

Evaluating price capping

There has been a great deal of discussion about the effectiveness of regulators such as Oftel and Ofwat and there are a number of problems associated with the price capping method they use:

- The relationship between the regulator and the privatised firm is characterised by asymmetric information. Regulators typically have fewer resources than the firm or firms they are trying to regulate and often find it difficult to obtain accurate information on costs. This makes it challenging to establish appropriate values for X.
- If the value of X is set too aggressively, it can lead to under-investment in the industry. A high value of X will mean low rates of return on investment in the future and discourage firms from taking the risk of putting money into new technology or greater capacity.
- A high value of X may encourage the firm to cut back on necessary expenditure in the name of efficiency gains. For example, there may be safety issues if maintenance expenditure is reduced.
- How long should the price capping formula last for? Usually, each cap is set for a 4 or 5 year period. If the period is too short, firms will face great uncertainty about the next value of X and investment may be adversely affected. If the period is too long, then any surprise efficiency gains will be kept by the firm as profits and not passed on to customers.

Examination skills and concepts

- Evaluating the use of price capping as a method of regulating privatised industries. For example, compare the UK method with the rate of return regulation (where companies are taxed a percentage of their profits) used by many other countries.
- Understanding the natural monopoly elements of many privatised industries. This makes regulation intrinsically difficult because there are no market benchmarks to go by.
- Discussing the optimal length of time for a price cap. Would it be a good idea for the regulator to change the value of X every year in the light of company profits?

Common examination errors

- A failure to understand the RPI minus X method of regulation. This has nothing to do with the RPIX measure of inflation targeted by the Bank of England's Monetary Policy Committee. Candidates need to be able to discuss the issues surrounding the calculation of X and be in a position to evaluate the use of this form of price capping.
- Writing in too general terms about the case study presented in the data–response. It is important to relate economic concepts to the question of privatisation. Terms such as supernormal profit, consumer surplus and allocative inefficiency should be used.

Useful exercises

- Build up a selection of newspaper articles on a privatised industry. Visit the websites of the company concerned and that of its regulator. Download and summarise any interesting articles. Be sure to build up a picture of how the chosen privatised industry is structured, the current price-capping regime and the recent performance of the firms involved.
- Search the internet for articles discussing the fate of Railtrack. Discuss with a friend whether the railways should ever have been privatised.

Linkages and common themes

- The topic of regulation allows the theory of monopoly to be applied to real examples. The basic natural monopoly framework applies quite closely to industries such as telecommunications and railways. The system of price capping attempts to produce the benefits of contestability in highly uncontestable markets.
- The link with other modules can be taken further. A regulator is there to establish a market, but asymmetric information may cause a market failure. Further, the regulator may just get things wrong and cause government failure.

Questions
&
Answers

This section has three supported multiple-choice question papers and three data–response questions. These questions are similar in style to the questions to be expected in the examination. Candidates are urged to attempt questions in this guide under timed conditions and to consult the answers only *after* making written responses.

With the supported multiple-choice questions, it is important to rehearse written explanations as well as choosing the correct answers. In the examination, each multiple-choice question is placed on a separate page with plenty of room for explanations. Wherever possible, draw diagrams to support written explanation.

Students can use the multiple-choice and data–response questions to check and reinforce understanding of the specification subject matter and to get used to answering questions under timed conditions.

This section also includes:

- Correct answers and explanations for the multiple-choice questions.
- Student answers varying between grade A and grade C for each data–response question.
- Examiner's comments on each data–response answer explaining, where relevant, how the answer could be improved and a higher grade achieved. These comments are preceded by the icon ℮.

Multiple-choice mark guide

Candidates are advised to spend approximately 35 minutes on the supported multiple-choice questions (leaving 5 minutes for checking, and 35 minutes for the data–response). There are ten multiple-choice questions on each paper, so there is a need to restrict time to no more than $3\frac{1}{2}$ minutes per question.

After selecting the answer, students need to justify their choice with a brief explanation. One mark is scored for each correct answer and another 3 marks are available for explanation.

Examiners apply the following rules when they are marking supported multiple-choice papers:
- If students get the answer wrong, they can still be awarded up to 2 out of 3 marks for explanation. For example, a correct definition of the key terms in the question may well pick up some marks. For this reason, it is vital not to leave any of the explanations blank.
- Students can score full marks for explaining the correct answer without reference to wrong answers. This is particularly important in Unit 4, because there is unlikely to be time to explain why the alternatives are wrong. However, students who think an explanation of the correct alternative is a bit thin could try to eliminate at least one answer.
- Students can score up to 2 marks out of 3 for eliminating wrong answers (usually 1 mark for each alternative eliminated successfully). This is therefore a useful strategy for candidates who are unsure about an explanation of the correct alternative or, indeed, unsure of the correct alternative itself.

Tips
- This first tip is worth repeating because it is so important. If at all possible, draw a diagram to support explanations. Some of the theoretical ideas included in the Unit 4 specification are difficult to express under timed conditions in an examination. Diagrams carry a lot of the explanation: use them, and include arrows marking the changes that have taken place.
- If asked to do a calculation, lay it out as if answering a maths problem. Start with the formula or definition. Then, on a separate line, fill in the numbers you have been given. Use further lines for simplification until you have the result.
- Candidates frequently score marks for marginal jottings which may have seemed to be of no use in the main answer. For example, if the reasoning includes a diagram, include it for the examiner and don't be satisfied with a tiny sketch in the corner of the page.
- Always define the key economic terms encountered in the question and correct answer. There are often marks reserved for this in the examiners' mark scheme. Failure to define key terms is one of the most common reasons for otherwise strong candidates dropping marks.

Multiple-choice questions

Paper 1

1 A reason why a firm might seek to grow in size would be to:
  A Reduce its market power
  B Ensure the existence of diseconomies of scale
  C Raise long-run average costs
  D Reduce labour productivity
  E Reduce long-run average costs

2 A firm's costs are given in the table below:

Quantity	Total cost
1	£100
2	£200
3	£300
4	£400

Which of the following is true for such a firm as it increases output?
  A Marginal costs rise and average costs fall
  B Average costs fall and marginal costs fall
  C Average costs rise and marginal costs rise
  D Average costs rise and marginal costs fall
  E Both average and marginal costs remain constant

3 A firm has average and marginal revenues as illustrated in the following diagram:

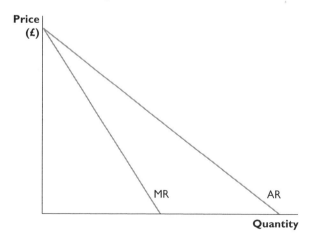

Which of the following statements is true for such a firm?

A Total revenue is falling as output increases

B As output increases, total revenue rises to the point where AR = 0

C As output increases, total revenue rises to the point where MR = 0

D As output increases, total revenue falls to the point where AR = 0

E As output increases, total revenue falls to the point where MR = 0

4 A restaurant finds that it can sell 30 fixed-priced lunches at £20 a meal. Reducing the price to £18 raises the demand to 31 meals. What is the restaurant's marginal revenue from the 31st lunch it sells?

A + £18

B + £2

C − £42

D − £60

E − £600

5 A profit-maximising firm will produce at a level of output where:

A Marginal revenue equals marginal cost

B Marginal revenue equals zero

C Marginal cost equals zero

D The firm is maximising sales

E The firm is charging the highest price possible

6 If Tesco made a successful takeover bid for the Waitrose supermarket chain, this would be an example of:

A Vertical integration

B Horizontal integration

C Conglomerate integration

D Freedom of entry

E Backward integration

7 The large sums of money spent by multinational companies promoting brands of shampoo such as Head and Shoulders and Timotei suggests that this market is:

A Nearly perfectly competitive

B Unlikely to be oligopolistic

C Unlikely to be contestable

D Likely to have a low five-firm concentration ratio

E Likely to be composed of firms which are price takers

8 If an airline charges different passengers different prices for the same seat on a plane, this is likely to be because:

A The company is making a loss

B An attempt is being made to ensure allocative efficiency

C An attempt is being made to ensure productive efficiency

D There are profits to be made from price discrimination

E The firm has adopted a revenue-maximising strategy

ultiple-choice questions

9 A privatised firm is regulated by the price-capping formula RPI minus X. If the regulator raises the value of X, this implies that:

A The regulator thinks that the firm is under too much market pressure

B The firm will be able to raise prices by no more than the new value of X%

C The firm is allowed to raise prices by X% above the rate of inflation

D The regulator believes that the firm could make greater efforts to cut costs

E There is little technological change in the industry

10 A profit-maximising monopoly will always be:

A Able to set price and output independently

B Allocatively efficient

C Productively efficient

D Unable to produce in the short run

E Able to set price or output but not both

Answers to multiple-choice questions Paper 1

Question 1
1 mark for correct answer E

One reason for the firm to grow is to achieve economies of scale. These are defined as falling long-run average costs. The firm may find its costs per unit falling as it expands the size of its factories. Examples of economies of scale include bulk-buying economies, marketing economies, the possibility of increased specialisation and volume economies. Be careful with the easy warm-up questions and do not forget to give basic terminology or definitions — in this case, economies of scale. It is always a good idea to give examples.

Question 2
1 mark for correct answer E

Define average cost (cost per unit of output) and marginal cost (cost of an extra unit of output). Calculate the cost per unit as total cost/quantity to give £100/1, £200/2 etc. = £100. Calculate the cost of an extra unit of output as the change in cost as output increases by one unit: £100 to £200, £200 to £300 etc., i.e. a marginal cost of £100. Once again, it is important to include the definitions and to give some explicit calculations.

Question 3
1 mark for correct answer C

Annotate the diagram as illustrated below. Show the total revenue curve (price × quantity) reaching a maximum where MR = 0.

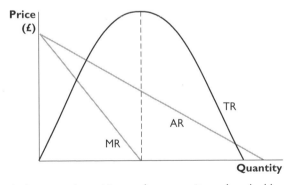

At first, marginal revenue is positive: each extra unit produced adds something positive to total revenue. After this, marginal revenue will be negative and so total revenue falls. Do not be afraid to make use of the diagrams and remember that annotations to these diagrams will count as part of an answer.

Question 4
1 mark for correct answer C

Marginal revenue is defined as the change in total revenue from selling one more unit of output. In this case, as the firm increases output from 30 to 31 it gains £18 from the 31st

lunch, but loses £2 on each of the previous lunches it was previously selling for £20. So the total change in revenue is £18 − £60 = −£42. In questions of this kind, there is no need to work out the total revenue figures (although this approach is perfectly acceptable). Simply calculate the changes at the margin.

Question 5
1 mark for correct answer A
Profit maximisation takes place at an output level where there is the greatest possible difference between total revenue and total cost. This occurs where marginal revenue equals marginal cost: that is, the revenue to be gained from selling an extra unit is equal to the cost of producing that unit. Beyond this point MC > MR, so an extra unit would add more to cost than to revenue and profit would fall. It is important to consider what is happening to profit just to the right or left of the maximising level of output.

Question 6
1 mark for correct answer B
Horizontal integration occurs where a firm merges with or acquires another company at the same stage of production as itself. In this case the two firms merging are both super-markets and they follow this rule. If Tesco had bought a farm to supply some of its produce, then this is at an earlier stage of production and the correct answer would be (backward) vertical integration. Sometimes there seems little to say when explaining the correct answer beyond the basic definition. In cases of this kind, be sure to explain why at least one of the other alternatives is wrong.

Question 7
1 mark for correct answer C
High levels of advertising are required to promote branded shampoos. These raise sunk costs of potential new entrants, and so make the industry less contestable. With only a few multinational firms, the market is oligopolistic and likely to have a high five-firm concen-tration ratio. Do not confuse concentration with competition. Low concentration implies many firms and high levels of competition.

Question 8
1 mark for correct answer D
Price discrimination occurs when a company sells the same product to different customers at different prices. The airline company's objective is to separate customers into groups willing to pay different prices, each group with different price elasticities of demand. If resale can be prevented, then the firm can capture consumer surplus and increase profits. It is helpful to talk about consumer surplus when explaining the concept of price discrimination.

Question 9
1 mark for correct answer D
The regulator must act as a surrogate for rival companies in a situation often close to being a natural monopoly. The price cap allows the firm to raise its price by no more than the rate of inflation less the value of X. By raising X, the regulator is signalling that it believes greater efficiency improvements are possible. It is sometimes useful to give a numerical example here based on the current rate of inflation and two different values of X.

Question 10

1 mark for correct answer E

Even monopolies are constrained by the market demand curve. Having chosen an output level at which MR = MC to profit maximise, the firm must then accept the price indicated by the demand curve. Otherwise, it would be unable to sell the quantity produced. This is a good example of a question where a diagram should be part of the explanation.

Multiple-choice questions

Paper 2

1 A contestable market is likely to be:
A Open to hit-and-run competition
B Vulnerable to tacit collusion
C Characterised by high barriers to entry
D Always composed of a large number of firms
E Always characterised by low levels of market concentration

2 The diagram shows a firm's marginal cost and marginal revenue curves:

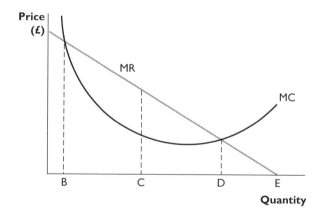

Which of the following statements is true for such a firm?
A The firm would profit maximise at B
B The firm would profit maximise at C
C The firm would profit maximise at D
D The firm would be allocatively efficient if it produced at E
E The firm would be sales maximising at E

3 The table below shows a firm's total revenue figures:

Output	Total revenue
10	£3,000
20	£6,000
30	£9,000
40	£12,000

Which of the following statements about this firm is correct?

A Marginal revenue is below average revenue

B Average revenue is below marginal revenue

C Both marginal and average revenue are falling

D Both marginal and average revenue are equal

E Both marginal and average revenue are equal to zero

4 A firm with positive marginal costs decides to adopt a policy of setting marginal revenue equal to zero. One motive for doing this would be to:

A Maximise profit

B Maximise revenue

C Maximise sales

D Minimise costs

E Minimise variable costs

5 The following table describes the situation of a market:

Number of firms	Long-run allocative efficiency	Long-run productive efficiency	Long-run profitability
Many	No	No	Normal

Which of the following market structures fits this data?

A Perfect competition

B Monopolistic competition

C Monopoly

D Oligopoly

E Duopoly

6 The emergence of cartel-like behaviour is most likely when an industry is characterised by:

A Diseconomies of scale at low levels of output

B The absence of sunk costs

C High levels of market concentration

D Low levels of vertical integration

E Low barriers to entry

7 A potential advantage of the 'RPI *minus* X' method of regulating privatised industries is that it:

A Guarantees that privatised firms will not be able to make supernormal profits

B Ensures that all pricing will be allocatively efficient

C Ensures that all pricing will be productively efficient

D Creates an incentive for firms to make no more than normal profit

E Creates an incentive for firms to make efficiency improvements

8 A firm seeking to reduce the contestability of an industry would:

A Adopt a policy of limit pricing

B Establish a high percentage mark-up over average costs

multiple-choice questions

    C Abandon any predatory pricing policies

    D Reduce advertising expenditure as a percentage of total costs

    E Adopt a policy of setting price equal to marginal cost

9 The Competition Commission uses the public interest criterion to judge whether a proposed merger should be allowed to go ahead. Which of the following would be a reason for blocking a merger?

    A The merger is unlikely to create regionally concentrated unemployment

    B The new firm is likely to be able to compete more effectively internationally

    C The merger would result in a loss of producer surplus

    D The new firm is likely to be in a position to conduct predatory pricing

    E The new firm would be small relative to the European market

10 Which of the following is most likely to be able to adopt a successful policy of price discrimination?

    A Newspaper sellers

    B Leading private surgeons

    C Beer producers

    D Confectionery retailers

    E Supermarkets

Answers to multiple-choice questions Paper 2

Question 1
1 mark for correct answer A
A contestable market is one with low levels of sunk costs. This means there are low barriers to exit for potential new entrants. If the incumbent firm is making supernormal profits in these circumstances, then entrepreneurs can employ hit-and-run tactics without much risk. There are low barriers to entry in such markets. The level of concentration is independent of the level of contestability. Even a monopoly can operate under contestable conditions, with the threat of new entrants forcing it to make no more than normal profit. Do not confuse contestability with market structure — it is an easy mistake to make.

Question 2
1 mark for correct answer C
Profit maximisation is where MR = MC. However, A is not the correct answer because to the right of B an extra unit adds more to revenue than to cost. At C, marginal profit is at its highest and adding an extra unit adds the most to profit. Only at D is marginal profit zero and total profit maximised. The condition MR = MC is a necessary but not a sufficient condition for profit maximisation. Note also that E, where MR = 0, is revenue maximisation, not sales maximisation.

Question 3
1 mark for correct answer D
Marginal revenue is the change in revenue from producing one more unit of output. In this example, total revenue rises by £3,000 for every 10 extra units, so MR = £300. Average revenue is the revenue per unit of output. Calculate this by dividing total revenue by output: in each case AR = £300. Be sure to read these questions carefully because it is easy to miss the qualifiers like marginal, average and total.

Question 4
1 mark for correct answer B
Marginal revenue is the revenue to be gained from selling one extra unit of output. If this is positive, the firm can increase output and total revenue will rise. If MR is negative, the firm can decrease output and total revenue will rise. Only where MR = 0 is total revenue at a maximum. This is another good example of a question where a diagram would be of help in the explanation.

Question 5
1 mark for correct answer B
Candidates should certainly draw a diagram to illustrate monopolistic competition (see overleaf). Each of the efficiency conditions and the fact that the firm is making only normal profit at Q_1 should be explained. This is a difficult diagram to draw in exam conditions and candidates should make sure they have prepared themselves.

multiple-choice questions

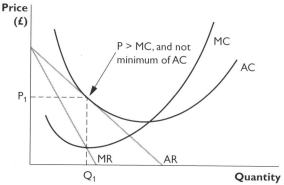

Monopolistic competition in the long run

Question 6

1 mark for correct answer C

A market has high levels of concentration when the largest five firms have a large percentage of sales. This will tend to make their decision-making interdependent and make price competition highly risky. The emergence of some form of collusion is likely. A cartel is an extreme form of such collusion, involving formal agreements to fix prices. Industries where firms have been caught colluding in recent years include cement and pharmaceuticals.

Question 7

1 mark for correct answer E

The RPI minus X formula needs to be explained: firms are allowed to raise prices by the rate of inflation less an amount X set by the regulator. However, if the firm can make efficiency improvements, it may be able to reduce costs faster than this cap on its price. Price capping allows the firm to keep any profits realised in this way. Do not confuse RPI minus X with the RPIX measure of inflation targeted by the Bank of England's Monetary Policy Committee.

Question 8

1 mark for correct answer A

Give a definition of contestability in terms of absence of sunk costs. To reduce contestability the firm will need to establish a reputation, so raising the perceived risk for new entrants. Limit pricing occurs where a firm is enjoying economies of scale and can use these as an opportunity to reduce price to forestall new entrants. Remember that candidates who think they have not said enough will find that eliminating wrong answers is a good strategy.

Question 9

1 mark for correct answer D

The Competition Commission would be concerned at the prospect of predatory pricing. This is when a firm reduces price in an attempt to drive other firms out of the market. If the merged firm has greater resources to fall back on, it will be able to survive a period of low prices better than its smaller rivals. From time to time, the national newspaper industry provides a good example of predatory pricing.

Question 10

1 mark for correct answer B

Private surgeons satisfy the conditions for price discrimination because people cannot sell an operation to someone else after they have had it. When people are seriously ill, they want treatment by a leading surgeon rather than a novice and it is possible for the surgeon to estimate price elasticity of demand. Supermarkets have sometimes been accused of charging higher prices where there are no local rivals but, generally, they do not discriminate. This question illustrates the principle that candidates should select the most likely answer.

Multiple-choice questions

Paper 3

1 Which of the following markets is closest to the model of perfect competition?
  A The market for second-hand cars
  B Supermarkets
  C The cocoa commodity market
  D The market for new computers
  E The railway industry

2 The diagram shows the total cost and total revenue curves of a monopoly:

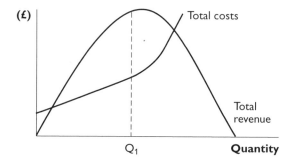

Q_1 indicates the quantity at which there is the greatest difference between total revenue and total costs. Which of the following statements is true at Q_1?
  A Marginal revenue is zero
  B Marginal revenue is maximised
  C The firm is making only normal profit
  D The firm could increase profit by making an extra unit of output
  E Marginal cost equals marginal revenue

3 The following diagram shows a profit-maximising monopolist:

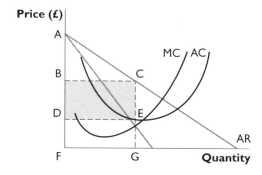

Which of the following areas shows the firm's total costs of production?

A ABC

B DEGF

C BCED

D BCGF

E DEGF minus ABC

4 The table below shows a firm's total cost and total revenue as output increases:

Output	Total cost	Total revenue
1	£200	£100
2	£300	£300
3	£390	£550
4	£460	£900

Which of the following statements is true for such a firm?

A Both marginal cost and marginal revenue are falling

B Both marginal cost and marginal revenue are rising

C Marginal cost is falling but marginal revenue is rising

D Marginal revenue is falling but marginal cost is rising

E Both marginal cost and marginal revenue are constant

5 Which of the following could be true for a firm in monopolistic competition?

A In the long run it could make a loss

B In the long run it could make supernormal profit

C In the short run it is only able to make normal profit

D In the short run it could make a loss

E It is a price taker in the short run but not in the long run

6 A UK regulatory body believes that a privatised firm is making supernormal profits. Which of the following is the regulator most likely to implement?

A A reduction in the value of X in the formula RPI minus X

B An increase in the length of the next price-capping period

C A tax on the profits of the firm

D Measures to make the industry more concentrated

E An increase in real price reductions in the next capping period

7 A bakery knows that at a price of 50p it will sell 10 doughnuts a day. To sell 11 doughnuts a day it finds that it needs to reduce price to 48p. What is the marginal revenue from the 41st doughnut?

A + 48p

B + 28p

C − 2p

D − 22p

E − 50p

ultiple-choice questions

8 Which of the following would indicate the existence of a contestable market?
A Persistently high supernormal profits
B High levels of allocative inefficiency
C Frequent hit-and-run entry
D High levels of productive inefficiency
E High levels of advertising expenditure

9 A computer assembly company acquires a microchip production company. This is an example of:
A Horizontal integration
B Forward vertical integration
C Backward vertical integration
D Conglomerate integration
E External economies of scale

10 Which of the following reasons for the merger in Question 9 is most likely to satisfy the Competition Commission that a merger should be allowed to go ahead?
A There are important technologies only currently available to one of the firms involved in the merger
B The merger is unlikely to produce any consequences for competition in the continental European market
C The companies involved have less than 40% market share and want to increase their market power
D There are important technologies only currently available to a firm not involved in the merger
E The degree of market concentration will be increased by the merger

Answers to multiple-choice questions Paper 3

Question 1
1 mark for correct answer C
The cocoa commodity market deals in a homogeneous good under conditions of near perfect information. Though entry is not completely costless, there are many buyers and sellers and there is freedom of entry and exit. The other products are heavily differentiated (e.g. computers) or monopolised (e.g. railways). Remember to go for the most likely answer because no industry completely matches the assumptions of perfect competition.

Question 2
1 mark for correct answer E
At Q_1 the gap between total revenue and total cost is greatest, and the firm is maximising profits. For this to be true MR = MC, i.e. the revenue from making an extra unit must be equal to the cost of producing an extra unit. Beyond Q_1, MC > MR (the slope of the total cost curve is greater than the slope of the total revenue curve), an extra unit would add more to cost than to revenue and the gap between TR and TC would be smaller. Always do a marginal analysis when explaining maximisation questions.

Question 3
1 mark for correct answer B
The firm is profit maximising where MR = MC, at output G. At this output level, the cost per unit is given by the average cost curve and is equal to the distance EG. Multiplying this by the quantity produced gives the total cost = DEGF. It is important with questions of this kind to derive the answer rather than just state it.

Question 4
1 mark for correct answer C
Marginal cost is the cost of an extra unit of output — the difference in total cost. In this case, marginal costs are £100, £90, £70 and falling. Marginal revenue is the extra revenue from selling one extra unit of output: in this case £200, £250, £350 and rising. Remember to give basic definitions and show evidence from the data in these questions.

Question 5
1 mark for correct answer D
Firms in monopolistic competition produce differentiated products in markets where there are many buyers and sellers, perfect information and freedom of entry and exit. This means that any supernormal profits made in the short run will be competed away in the long run, when only normal profits can be made. The diagram (overleaf) shows that in the short run it is quite possible for the firm to make a loss, e.g. after a fall in demand. At the profit-maximising level of output, the firm is making a loss per unit of GH, which when multiplied by the quantity produced gives the total loss represented by the shaded area. Some firms will then leave the industry until the surviving firms are once again making normal profits. This is a good example of a question where a diagram is the best way to make a convincing explanation.

multiple-choice questions

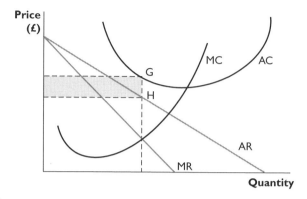

Question 6
1 mark for correct answer E
UK regulators use the formula RPI minus X. This allows the firm to raise prices by no more than the rate of inflation less an amount X which represents the efficiency improvements the regulator believes the company to be capable of. In this case, the firm is making super-normal profits so the value of X is likely to be raised in the next capping period, thus increasing the real price reduction imposed on the firm.

Question 7
1 mark for correct answer B
Marginal revenue is the change in total revenue from producing one more unit of output. In this case, the firm gains 48p for the eleventh doughnut sold but loses 2p on each of the ten previously sold at 50p. So the change in total revenue is 48p – 20p = 28p. This method is generally quicker than working out the total revenues and taking the difference between them.

Question 8
1 mark for correct answer C
Give a definition of a contestable market in terms of low sunk costs implying low barriers to entry and exit. This allows hit-and-run entry, which is entering a market to capture supernormal profit before leaving without cost because of the absence of sunk costs. All the other answers involve the presence of sunk costs (e.g. advertising) or indicate the inefficiencies of incumbent firms that are not worried about the appearance of new rivals.

Question 9
1 mark for correct answer C
Backward vertical integration occurs where a firm buys a company at an earlier stage in the chain of production than itself, as with microchips in the production of computers. This may allow the firm to keep better control on costs by cutting out the margins of dis-tributors. Be sure to refer to the actual industry given in the question.

Question 10
1 mark for correct answer D
The Competition Commission must assess whether the proposed merger is in the public interest. If a firm in the industry has exclusive access to an important technology, then the

industry may rapidly cease to be competitive. A merger by other firms may be the only way to ensure some competition in the future. This is probably a good example of a question where eliminating some of the wrong answers would be a productive strategy.

Data–response questions
Question 1
The record industry

Where have all the good times gone? Michael Jackson, Mariah Carey, Mick Jagger and REM used to be the guaranteed money-spinners of the global music business. But not any more.

Sony Music spent a rumoured £41 million getting Jacko into the studio to record *Invincible*, an album that proved he was anything but. It had sold less than 6 million copies by the end of last year. EMI paid £38 million to end its short but nightmarish relationship with Mariah Carey, the once multi-platinum pop diva whose last album, *Glitter*, sold just 2 million copies. And REM, signed by Warner Music for an estimated $80 million, have had $3 million worth of marketing behind their new album and still only sold just over 3 million.

This year, the global recorded music business is set to shrink for the sixth consecutive year. It is estimated that recorded music sales will fall from $36.9 billion in 2000 to $31.8 billion in 2003. With little to sing about when it comes to near-term revenue growth, EMI this week sought to appease investors by dealing with the other half of the equation: costs. It announced 1,800 job cuts — 20% of the workforce — to achieve nearly £100 million in annual cost savings. It also knocked a quarter of its acts off the company's roster.

'There are some real challenges facing the music industry at the moment,' admits Alain Levy, the head of recorded music at EMI who has overseen the restructuring. 'We are positioning EMI for revenue growth from a much lower cost base.'

Another London-based music executive puts it more brutally: 'If you walked into the City of London and asked for money to start a record label, you would probably get a less welcome reception than if you wanted to set up a dotcom.'

But no amount of corporate re-engineering can get around the fact that the music business is about panning for gold. As one veteran says: 'You can cut only so far and then you simply have to start selling records.'

Mr Levy says the music business 'has lost its magic'. Michael, Mariah and Mick, it seems, have lost theirs too.

Source: *Financial Times*, 23 March 2002.

(a) **Using a diagram, analyse the effect on price and output of a record company experiencing a fall in demand for its product.** (6.marks)

(b) **With reference to the passage, evaluate one source of finance to a record company.** (4 marks)

(c) **Assess ways in which a record producer could try to increase sales of its product.** (10 marks)

(d) **To what extent is lack of contestability in the record industry likely to mean that firms are able to achieve supernormal profits?** (10 marks)

(e) **Assess the likely benefits two record companies would get from agreeing to merge.** (10 marks)

■ ■ ■

Candidate's answer

(a) The record producer will face a downward-sloping demand curve because it sells a differentiated product in circumstances where there is a restricted number of producers. As demand falls the AR curve shifts to the left, as does the associated MR curve. The profit-maximising level of output is where MR = MC as this is where marginal profit is zero. As illustrated on the diagram below, output therefore falls and so does price.

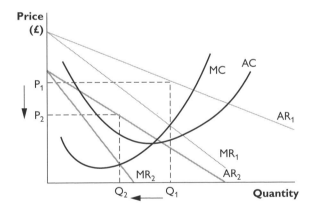

A profit-maximising monopolist

6/6 marks

✒ This is an excellent answer. The candidate has obeyed the instruction to draw a diagram, and has labelled it clearly. The shift in AR is matched correctly by a shift in MR. The arrows on the axes make it clear what is going on.

(b) The company could raise money by asking for a bank loan, using its assets as collateral. However, this may be a fairly expensive source of finance and it would be cheaper to use internally generated finance. **2/4 marks**

e This is a reasonable answer, which has the merit of evaluating the chosen method of finance. However, the candidate has failed to obey the question's instructions and use the example from the passage — in this case, raising money from the City.

(c) A record producer could use a number of price and non-pricing strategies to try to increase sales. Advertising influences record sales and the firm could widen its marketing strategy to cover outlets such as the internet. However, the passage states that Warner spent $3 million advertising REM and the increase in sales was disappointing. The firm could make special offers such as competitions, tokens to collect and exchange for free CDs or other prizes. However, the fall in demand has been so great that these may be of limited use. They usually work as a means of maintaining rather than increasing demand.

An alternative approach to raising sales would be to cut prices. The effectiveness of this strategy depends, however, on the price elasticity of demand. If demand is inelastic, the price-cutting strategy will fail. The reactions of rival companies will also be very important. There are only a few major record producers, so cutting prices might risk a price war. **8/10 marks**

e Here is a good answer where the candidate has covered both price and non-price competition. A notable feature of the answer is that it attempts to evaluate each of the chosen policies rather than just list them. There could, however, have been more on alternative pricing strategies.

(d) Contestability is where an industry has no barriers to entry and therefore where new firms can enter and take away supernormal profit from the incumbent firms. The record industry is likely to have many barriers to entry. These include the large scale of production of the multinational companies already in the industry, which means they will have lower average costs than any new entrant. Economies of scale include marketing, volume and overcoming indivisibilities. On the other hand, it is possible for even a small record producer to make supernormal profit if it is lucky enough to sign a band that turns out to be successful. **4/10 marks**

e This is a weak answer. It gets off to a bad start because it fails accurately to define the concept of contestability. The lack of reference to sunk costs means the answer cannot develop the concept of hit-and-run entry. The candidate also fails to mention the role of advertising — probably the largest sunk cost in this industry. There is plenty of evidence in the passage that the record industry is not very profitable, but the candidate does not use this evidence. On the other hand, there are some reasonable points and these are related to the industry in the article.

(e) This would be an example of horizontal integration where both the companies involved are at the same stage of production. Record producers could realise a number of different benefits from this kind of merger. There may be synergies from merging catalogues of records and being able to offer fuller lists of artists in certain categories or just a wider variety of categories. However, many labels exist successfully as niche products. There will clearly be advertising economies discussed in my previous answer.

On the production side, a merger gives the companies a reason for rationalising management by cutting out unnecessary layers of junior executives who tend to be paid high salaries in the record industry. Only one board of directors will be required to run what were two companies and this should reduce administration costs. **6/10 marks**

In this reasonable answer the candidate begins well with a discussion of horizontal integration. There is plenty of application to the record industry rather than just a list of potential economies of scale. The candidate should not, however, refer to previous answers because the answer given must stand or fall by itself. There are many grade-A sections in this answer, but the performance is just a little too uneven to justify a grade A overall.

Scored: 26/40 = grade B

Question 2
Newspaper sales and competition policy

It's hardly news to anyone who reads the papers that advertising has slumped seriously these past few months. Like the rest of the press, Daily Mail and General Trust (DMGT), which publishes the *Evening Standard* and *Metro*, the *Mail* and its Sunday sister, has hardly been jumping for joy.

As well as the big full-page advertisements that we all usually think of, its job advertising is down because no one is recruiting staff. Yesterday's trading statement showed that things were slightly better than expected, with display advertising for February down 8% on last year, compared with post-September 11 slumps in the region of 16%.

However, Peter Williams, the DMGT finance director, said yesterday that he does not expect advertising to pick up in this calendar year.

The exposure to *Euromoney*, in which DMGT has a 70% stake, is also worrying. The financial publishing house is suffering terribly and will be slower to bounce back.

That's not great, but DMGT says it can handle it. The company has managed its way through several recessions and is yet to cut any staff. Recent cover price hikes sailed through without affecting circulation. DMGT has a lot of slack that its rivals do not.

The company's portfolio is diverse and the management respected. The share price has remained relatively constant this year, closing yesterday at 698p. No need for Irritable Mail Syndrome just yet.

Source: *Daily Telegraph*, 15 March 2002.

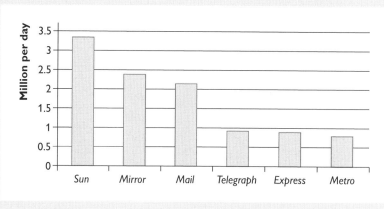

Daily newspaper sales

(a) (i) What does the passage suggest about the price elasticity of demand
for newspapers? (4 marks)
(ii) Explain the significance of this information to the pricing strategies of
companies such as **DMGT**. (6 marks)
(b) Evaluate the use of non-price competition by newspaper companies. (6 marks)
(c) The ownership of the *Evening Standard* currently gives **DMGT** a local
monopoly in the provision of daytime newspapers to the London region.
Assess reasons why there is only one company operating in this market. (12 marks)
(d) To what extent would a merger between newspaper groups be likely to be
of concern to the competition authorities? (12 marks)

■ ■ ■

Candidate's answer

(a) (i) The price elasticity of demand is defined as the percentage change in quantity
demanded divided by the percentage change in price. The passage says 'recent
cover price hikes sailed through without affecting circulation' and this suggests
that demand for the DMGT newspapers is price inelastic, as illustrated in the
following diagram:

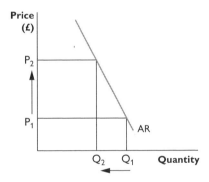

The diagram shows that when the price of newspapers is raised by x% the
quantity demanded falls by less than x%, raising the total revenue of producers.
4/4 marks

✍ This is an ideal answer. It is important with such questions not to forget to include
the definition, which in this case is worth 2 out of the 4 marks available.

(ii) This suggests that at current price levels DMGT can raise prices. Because
demand is inelastic, when price is raised the percentage fall in demand should
be less than the percentage increase in price. Revenue — which is price multiplied by quantity — should therefore increase. Meanwhile, a small fall in
demand will leave the company's costs virtually unchanged so, other things
remaining the same, profits should increase. **4/6 marks**

✍ The candidate has the correct answer. However, a diagram to illustrate the point
would have ensured full marks. It is also necessary to point out that the firm

cannot just keep raising prices to raise revenue: at some point demand will become elastic as the firm moves up the demand curve.

(b) Newspapers use many forms of non-price competition. The most effective form is probably national advertising, often on TV. This reaches a large audience but is quite expensive. Newspapers often run competitions to encourage customer loyalty. They also run promotions such as collecting a series of tokens to eat cheaply in restaurants. Though this can encourage repeat buying, many customers ignore such offers. Newspapers also compete by differentiating their product through adopting a particular political point of view or offering a better range of supplementary sections. The passage states that this newspaper company publishes more than one title and this allows it to segment the market. However, to what extent these forms of non-price competition are more effective than price competition is hard to judge. **6/6 marks**

ℓ This is a good answer because it is applied directly to the question and makes good use of illustrative experience of the actual product, rather than just talking in generalities.

(c) The main reason why there is only one daytime newspaper in London is probably the size of the market. In national newspaper terms, the London market is quite small. With high costs of production and a limited market there may be a niche for only one newspaper.

The *Evening Standard* has been around for some time, so it enjoys a strong reputation, both among customers and advertisers. This raises the risk of new entry to entrepreneurs thinking of starting up new titles. The extensive advertising and promotions conducted by the *Standard* raise the sunk costs of potential new entrants and make the market less contestable.

From time to time, the *Evening Standard* has had temporary price cuts to stimulate sales. This also serves the purpose of raising the risk for new entrants. A new entrant might also find difficulty establishing a distribution network for the new title. **7/12 marks**

ℓ This has the makings of a good answer, with many relevant points identified. However, the candidate has rather glossed over the evaluation side of the question. In this case, 4 of the 12 marks available were for examining the relative significance of the factors discussed or for making other critical comment.

(d) The Competition Commission has the power to investigate any merger involving more than 25% market share. Newspaper groups in the UK are large relative to the size of the market, as the bar chart in the question makes clear. Therefore, any proposed merger is likely to be investigated.

The role of the Competition Commission is to judge whether the merger would be in the public interest. It is likely that the most significant factor to concern the Commission would be the effect of a merger on prices. With fewer titles, it would be tempting for newspaper proprietors to raise cover prices substantially. This would reduce consumer surplus.

The impact on consumer choice might be judged as equally important. Newspapers are a key vehicle of free speech in a democratic society, and it is important that a range of views is expressed. This may be less likely if all the titles are owned by one company.

Probably of less significance would be the impact on employment. There is a general shortage of labour in London, where many newspapers are based, so any workers sacked as a result of the merger would be likely to be absorbed in other occupations. **10/12 marks**

The candidate provides a strong answer where the newspaper market has been used explicitly, with a number of public interest issues considered and evaluated. Issues like the relationship between newspapers and television might also have been discussed. Overall, this is a strong answer with good application of economic concepts, secure definitions and — for the most part — a high level of evaluation.

Scored: 31/40 = grade A

Question 3

Regulation of privatised industries

Regulators of privatised companies running the pipes and wires delivering Britain's essential services are achieving lower prices and improved efficiency, according to a report published today by the National Audit Office.

However, the independent public spending watchdog says the system of capping prices charged by monopoly transmission providers could be improved by providing greater certainty and transparency over future capital spending requirements and investment returns.

Ofwat, the water regulator, was heavily criticised by companies for big price cuts imposed in April 2000, which they said severely weakened their ability to finance large investment programmes to improve water quality and protect the environment.

But the report praises Ofwat, Ofgem (the energy industry regulator) and Oftel (the telecommunications regulator) for delivering 'lower prices and high-quality services' while encouraging companies 'to cut costs and invest'.

'Without some form of regulatory intervention, there is a risk that companies in a monopoly or strongly dominant market position would be able to set excessive prices or to provide a lower quality of service,' it said. This is particularly true in the water industry where there are strong natural monopoly elements to the market structure.

It concluded that setting price caps every 4 to 5 years, using the RPI minus X formula, had mostly worked well: 'In the most recent reviews, regulators introduced price cuts for customers of network companies ranging from 1.5% for electricity transmission to 13% for telecommunications.'

Regulatory period	Values of X
1989–1991	4.50
1991–1993	6.25
1993–1997	7.50
1997–2002	4.50

Recent BT price caps

Source: *Financial Times*, 10 April 2002.

(a) Using a diagram, explain what is meant by 'natural monopoly elements' in the
market for water. (6 marks)
(b) With reference to the data, explain the system of price capping based on the
RPI minus **X** formula. (6 marks)
(c) Examine two reasons why Oftel reduced the value of **X** in 1997. (10 marks)
(d) Assess the advantages of having a longer price-capping period than 5 years. (6 marks)
(e) Evaluate the use of price capping as a method of regulating the
privatised industries. (12 marks)

■ ■ ■

Candidate's answer

(a) A natural monopoly has falling long-run average costs (LRAC) at all conceivable
levels of output, as illustrated in the diagram:

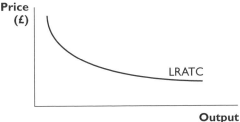

In the case of the water industry, there are the high fixed costs of installing reser-
voirs and pipelines. These form a large proportion of total costs and so average
costs fall as output increases, allowing the firm to spread its fixed costs per unit
more thinly. **5/6 marks**

🖉 This is a good answer where the concept of natural monopoly is correctly defined
and the diagram is accurate and labelled properly. It could also have shown marginal
costs (below average costs) and the profit-maximising level of output. There is
good application to the context of the water industry.

(b) Price capping is a method of regulating privatised industries. It is a system based
on reducing the amount by which companies are allowed to raise their prices. The
RPI minus X method allows price increases of no more than the rate of inflation
less an amount X set by the regulator, e.g. Ofgem. The value of X is determined
according to the efficiency improvements the regulator thinks the company would
have made had it been in a more competitive market environment. The greater
the efficiency improvements the regulator thinks possible, the higher the value of
X and the greater the company's real reduction in prices. **4/6 marks**

🖉 Here is a good example of how an excellent answer can nonetheless drop marks
unnecessarily. The question said 'with reference to the data' and the candidate
makes no such reference. All that was required was to apply the concept to, say,
the RPI minus 4.5% example in the table.

ata–response question 3

(c) In 1997 Oftel reduced the value of X from 7.5% to 4.5%. The first reason for this was probably that the regulator felt there was greater competition in the industry. This was mainly due to technological change and the development of alternative ways of transmitting phone calls. With more competitors, the heat would be on BT to keep its prices low or risk losing market share. Regulators are only required if there are monopolies to deal with. Optical cables and satellites, and the development of mobile phones, has meant that Oftel has less need to worry that BT might abuse what used to be considerable market power.

The second reason was that Oftel must have believed BT to be capable of making further efficiency improvements in terms of raising labour productivity. The price cap is designed to encourage the directors of BT to find ways of improving working practices or of introducing cost-cutting investment.

Of these, I believe that the former is the most important. BT had already made considerable cuts to the number of its employees in the years immediately following privatisation. There is unlikely to be all that much room for more efficiency improvements. **8/10 marks**

> This is an excellent answer with good use of other knowledge and a clear command of the basic concepts. Does the detail tail off a bit towards the end?

(d) The problem with this question is 'advantages' to whom? Clearly, if the cap were reasonable, the company would like to enjoy longer periods of price capping. A longer cap allows the company to keep all the profits it makes by increasing efficiency faster than the regulator thought possible when setting the value of X. This may also have advantages to customers. The investment confidence of the company may be increased because uncertainty about prices will be reduced by the longer capping period.

On the downside, the longer period means that if the regulator underestimates the efficiency savings that are possible, then consumers will have to put up with prices that are higher than they need to be for the whole period of the cap. Regulators have occasionally intervened mid-period to review X but this creates enormous uncertainty in the industry. **6/6 marks**

> The candidate has a clear understanding of this issue and evaluates critically the idea of longer price-capping periods by looking at the disadvantages as well as the advantages.

(e) Price capping is said to have many advantages over other systems of regulating privatised industries such as the rate of return method used in the US. By allowing the company to keep any profits made under the cap, an incentive is created to cut costs as much as possible. However, this assumes the directors of the company are profit maximisers. A constant value of X over a 4 or 5 year period maintains a certain degree of stability in the industry, and this could allow firms to make risky investment decisions.

However, the system has been criticised. The first — and major — problem is that of regulatory capture. Unfortunately, there is a tendency for regulators to fall under the sway of the companies they are meant to be regulating. This is mainly because of the problem of asymmetric information where regulators often do not have the necessary information to make sound decisions about the value of X. This creates a second problem: the value of X may turn out to be too generous or too strict. If it is the former, then the firm will make supernormal profits at the expense of the consumer; if the latter, then investment and growth in the firm may be artificially restricted.   **9/12 marks**

✍ This well-crafted answer presents the advantages of the RPI minus X system. Some major disadvantages are discussed and a clear conclusion drawn, and so the candidate qualifies for evaluation marks. It would have been helpful if the candidate had drawn from a real example such as the controversy over capping in the electricity and water industries. This is a competent performance by a well-prepared candidate.

Scored 32/40 = grade A